Mary Cook's
THIS THEN
WAS HOME

Published by Creative Bound Inc.
www.creativebound.com

ISBN 978-0-921165-89-7
Printed and bound in Canada

Book design by Wendelina O'Keefe, Creative Bound International Inc.

Cover illustration, original art by Rosemary Leach

Library and Archives Canada Cataloguing in Publication

Cook, Mary, 1932-
      This then was home / Mary Cook ; original illustration by Rosemary Leach.
ISBN 978-0-921165-89-7
      1. Cook, Mary, 1932- —Childhood and youth—Anecdotes. 2. Farm
life—Ontario—Renfrew (County). 3. Renfrew (Ont. : County)—Biography.
I. Title.
FC3095.R4Z49 2007   971.3'8103'092   C2007-906361-6

Dedication

To all those who cherish their memories, enjoy cooking, and occasionally spin tales of their own, I dedicate this book. And to all those who have supported and encouraged me over the decades—and you know who you are—I give my heartfelt thanks and appreciation.

A celebrated storyteller, **Mary Cook** has been delighting Canadian audiences for years with her remembrances of growing up on the family farm during the bittersweet years of the 1930s. She is a regular contributor to newspapers and magazines across the country, and is the author of ten best-selling books, including *Liar, Liar, Pants on Fire*, *Another Place at the Table* and *A Bubble off Plumb*.

Mary has received seven Actra awards for excellence in broadcast journalism, during an illustrious career that began 50 years ago with the CBC in Windsor, Ontario, and spanned 25 years in Ottawa. Most recently, she has been a regular guest on CBC's "Fresh Air," recorded in Toronto. By the time this book has gone to press, Mary will have launched a regular segment on Valley Heritage Radio, 98.7, in Renfrew, Ontario.

Contents

A Note from the Author

It would seem to me that, after ten books, further explanation may be required to justify why those characters first introduced thirty years ago are still central to the storyline in my writings. The simple truth is that they have become as familiar as your own backyard. Those who have visited the pages of my books are well acquainted with Marguerite, Cecil, Joyce, Velma, and my large extended family. They know the Northcote Side Road as well as I do, and I daresay, when you mention Briscoe's General Store to my readers, they can picture the kegs of nails sitting right alongside the boxes of maple cookies, and can visualize the bolts of printed fabric stacked on the plank shelves.

I am continually asked if the characters on my pages are real people. My answer is that the characters are as real as you, the reader, want to make them. Oh, there really are a Cecil and a Joyce, and after many decades not only do they appear regularly on my pages, but we touch base often enough to keep our lifelong friendships alive. I admit to creating some colourful characters who blend in well with the theme of a story, and situations do develop that require embellishment. But when I meet with old friends and we talk about that bittersweet era, the Depression years, we invariably get into a "mind the time" mode, and therein another story is born.

In this, my eleventh book, you will meet some new faces, and revisit many of those whom you have loved or hated for the past thirty years. My nemesis Marguerite will always have a place in my storytelling. I would like to say she has mellowed, or that I have become more tolerant and less envious of the young girl who often succeeded in making my life miserable, but alas, Marguerite hasn't changed, nor has she taken on a gentler, kinder persona.

Cecil will surface as the class mischief maker he has always been, right along with my brother Emerson and my cousin Ronny. Alone, each was someone to be reckoned with. Together, they created havoc. Joyce will still be the perfect little classmate who had everything going for her, and yet accepted me as a friend, in spite of her family's relative wealth. Velma will still be the little friend who lived on the next farm, shared her lunch with me, and walked the three and a half miles home with me every day from the Northcote School.

Often my characters will emerge as something other than perfect little models of decorum, and I may have used their proper names, while making them into characters not exactly true to their real personalities. At other times, fictitious names will surface, wrapped around a very true happening or circumstance. But at all times, I have tried to paint a picture of what it was like to grow up on a not-too-productive farm during the 1930s, surrounded by a loving family, and a warm and caring community. It was an era where deals were made with the simple shake of a hand, and a man's word was his bond. And a time when Saturday night house parties and a weekly trip into town to sit on the main street and watch the world go by, were entertainment enough for us.

So let me take you back to a more gentle time again, and allow me to reintroduce those beloved characters, some real, some imaginary, and take you back to roads on which you have travelled before. Come with me to a time when, with the Depression closing in around them, a strong community of people emerged, leaving a legacy of honesty and integrity to my generation. These then are the stories of a people who knew that only from the sweat of their own brows could they survive, and overcome, the toughest of times. When they looked over their lands they did not see defeat, they saw fields rich with dreams.

Mary

This Then Was Home

It did little good for Mother to complain about the shortcomings of that old log house we lived in, in Northcote. There was no money for making improvements for one thing, and for another, Father said any house that had served one family for three generations didn't need any "fixin' up," as he called it.

There were only three rooms downstairs, the largest being the kitchen which was divided from the parlour by a staircase. Mother said the parlour was not much good for anything other than collecting dust and holding the family bible that sat on a shaky twig table under the only window in the room.

Almost as an afterthought, a small room jutted out from the kitchen and held a double bed, a small dresser and one overstuffed chair that served as a resting place for Father's work clothes when he undressed at night.

Upstairs there were only two tiny bedrooms, and a hall that served as a bedroom for my sister Audrey and me. The other two rooms were so small that my three brothers moved from one to the other on a regular basis, because in one there was a cot, and in the other something that resembled a double bed but which was, in fact, much smaller. They changed beds on Mother's orders because she thought it only fair that they each had a shot at the cot, the more comfortable of the two.

There were no clothes closets in the entire house, so narrow boards were nailed to the back of the bedroom doors to hold our clothes. Each board held four spikes. That was one thing that drove Mother to distraction! "I'm sure every house in Renfrew has a clothes closet," she lamented. Father pointed out that building clothes closets in any room in the house would cut the space down by half. So the two-by-fours were all we had as long as we lived in Northcote.

The peaked roof allowed for wide board ceilings upstairs, which were whitewashed every year, and it wasn't unusual to be lying in bed and feel flakes of dried whitewash fall on your face. In the summertime, the tarpaper roof attracted the heat, making the bedrooms blisteringly hot. In the winter we could see hoarfrost on the ceiling boards. A silver-painted stovepipe snaked through the hall and supplied the only heat to the entire upstairs. When we crawled out of bed in the winter, we could see our breath.

There was no foundation under that old log house, so every winter Father packed snow all around the outside. He said it kept the house warmer. Mother didn't believe him for a minute. The floors were cold and drafty, and the small windowpanes became covered with frost early in the winter, making it impossible to see outside. Although Mother always said pine and poverty went well together, the baseboards, wainscoting, door and window frames were wide pine, which she hated with a passion. The house, built more than a hundred years before Mother came to it, had all the earmarks of a pioneer home—a far cry from the apartment she had left in New York City, with its running water, electricity and telephone.

Mother complained about the old log house, but nonetheless was able to make it into a cheery and cosy home. Braided rugs were everywhere, curtains were made from bleached flour bags, and pictures taken from calendars hung in every room. The big Findlay Oval stove dominated the kitchen, and Mother was finally able to master it after many failed suppers and aprons scorched from standing too close to the firebox. Early in the summer it was dismantled, and with an effort that included everyone in the entire house, it was transferred to the summer kitchen, where it would get its annual scrubbing down, and have its stovepipes painted shiny silver. Moving it out of the kitchen helped keep the rest of the house cool when the unrelenting summer sun beat down on the roof, penetrating the walls.

Although now, so many years later, I wonder at the primitive conditions under which we lived, I remember too the warmth from that old log house. Not just warmth from the summer sun and the Findlay Oval, but from a house bursting with five active children, neighbours coming for card games and Saturday night house parties, the wonderful smells of homemade bread, and sap boiling on the back of the stove, and gum rubbers drying out propped against a stick of wood.

I remember the sounds of that house. Mother on the treadle Singer sewing machine, the frost cracking the logs of the house on a cold winter's night, the big shiny kettle always simmering on the back burner of the Findlay Oval, Father stirring before daybreak to start the stove.

I see in my mind's eye the old cretonne couch in one corner of the kitchen where Father took a noon nap, the balls of string at the ready for idle hands to turn into dish cloths, and the tin matchbox that hung at the back door and held a large box of matches bought at Briscoe's General Store for a dime. I can see the blue sugar bowl where Mother kept her "egg money" for a hoped-for trip back to see New York City just one more time...the trip that would never be, and I see joyful times and prayers around my mother's knee. And I know that even though we were poor in material trappings, we were very rich in spirit inside the walls of that place we called home.

Winter Magic

It only happened in the wintertime. And always on a Saturday night. And, of course, the conditions had to be ideal. The weather, Father would say, was taking a turn for the worse. That meant more snow, and then freezing rain on top of that. While Father brooded over the elements, we five children would secretly rejoice. Father was concerned that the horse would slip on the icy roads and break a leg. And so until the ice melted, we had to stay close to home, relying on the pantry for staples, the root cellar for our vegetables, the smokehouse for our meat, and Mother's talent for using what was on hand to put a hearty meal on the table.

The ideal conditions we children waited for were the heavy and continuous snowfall, followed by freezing rain that would turn the fields and barnyard into an endless surface of frozen magic. And when that happened, we children prayed for a moonlit night. My sister Audrey would check the *Farmer's Almanac* and say, "Yes, we are in luck. The moon is going to be full." And then there would be such excitement we could hardly contain ourselves. I didn't know how we would ever wait until

Saturday night. And it was that waiting that added to the anticipation of what was ahead.

There was little chance of going far from the farm on an icy winter's night. Even the Saturday night house parties would be put on hold until the weather permitted. But Mother had a special talent for making the most simple of pleasures into a joyous occasion.

When the conditions were just perfect—the heavy snow followed by freezing rain, and the moon at its fullest on a Saturday night—it was a time for magic. The room my sister and I shared at the top of the stairs was the only room with two windows: one close to the landing, and the other in the middle of the room. The stovepipe from the Findlay Oval snaked through a hole in the floor.

On that special Saturday night we would haul extra kitchen chairs upstairs after we had cleaned away the supper dishes and tidied everything to Mother's satisfaction. The chairs were placed in front of the windows, and even though the stovepipe was supposed to give off enough heat to make the bedrooms comfortable, it was never warm enough to suit me. And so, when we each took a chair in front of a window, Mother would take blankets off the beds and wrap one around each of us, making sure there was a good tuck-in for our feet. And then she would go downstairs and we could hear her in the kitchen getting ready for the next step on this night of magic.

Father thought the whole idea of sitting at a window looking out at snow and ice was just about the craziest thing he ever heard of. He could be found instead sitting in the rocking chair, with his feet on a cushion on the open oven door of the Findlay Oval, reading the *Ottawa Farm Journal*.

While we sat gazing out the window, Mother would come upstairs with a tray holding cups of hot chocolate and sugar cookies that she would have made especially for the occasion. Once we had our hands wrapped securely around our cups, she would blow out the coal-oil lamp, and it would take a few seconds for our eyes to adjust to the darkness of the room.

And then we would look out the windows at that special night, with the ice-covered fields as far as our eyes could see, and even the West Hill would be coated and glistening in the moonlight. It was as if someone had come out to Northcote and laid a blanket of stardust over the entire countryside. With the moon so bright, and the sky lit up with a million stars, we were in another land.

Mother would pull a chair up behind us and, in her beautiful soft voice, would set the stage for that night of magic. I would shiver with delight, and a bit of fear, as she told us stories of make-believe. They were tales of unheard-of lands, of people who could fly with magic wings, and animals that could talk. One story I remember especially, was of a huge bird with white feathers that could sing in several languages—a necessity, since it had to go to many countries throughout the world and visit children of every nationality!

The stories would be interrupted when she stopped suddenly to tell us to look closely beyond the West Hill and see if we could count the diamonds in the fields. And with the moon so bright, and only the shadows of the trees breaking the expanse of icy snow, we would pretend that we were counting real diamonds. Audrey would start, and when she got tired, one of the brothers would take over. Finally, it would be my turn. But by this time my eyes would be heavy, and I would rest my head on Audrey's shoulder, and I never knew how it happened, but I would awaken the next morning in my bed, and the night of magic would be over.

At a time when there was no money to go to the picture show in Renfrew, and the weather prevented us from visiting neighbours or having them come for an evening of cards and music, Mother was able to create for us a wonderful night of entertainment and enchantment. I fully believed that the Depression was happening in some other land, and that we were just about the wealthiest family in Renfrew County.

From the Apple Barrel

Bread pudding was no treat to me back in those Depression years. It appeared too often on our table when there was little else in the cupboard for dessert. But at this time of year, when the apple barrel was still fairly full of fall apples, Mother made a wonderful marbled apple cake. It had no specific name; we just called it Mother's special apple cake. I especially liked helping to make it, because I was allowed to get all the Watkins spices down from the kitchen cupboard to put into the cake. These were spices bought from the Watkins man who came right to the door with suitcases of everything from liniments to spices to kitchen gadgets. This recipe is quite spicy, so you may prefer to cut down on the cloves.

Recipe, next page

Mother's Special Apple Cake

4 cups	fall apples, pared and sliced	1 litre
	(Mother left the skins on—heaven forbid that any of the	
	apple be wasted!— but I usually peel the apples.)	
1 cup	white sugar	250 ml
1– 2 tbsp	flour	15–30 ml
1 tsp	cinnamon	5 ml
2 tbsp	butter	30 ml
2 tbsp	water	30 ml
1 tbsp	lemon juice	15 ml
	(My addition...we couldn't afford lemons back in the '30s.)	
2 1/4 cups	sifted flour	550 ml
2 tsp	baking powder	10 ml
1 tsp	ginger	5 ml
1/2 tsp	salt	2 ml
1/2 cup	shortening	125 ml
1 cup	sugar	250 ml
2	eggs	2
2/3 cup	milk	150 ml
1/4 cup	molasses	50 ml
1/4 tsp	soda	1 ml
1 tsp	cinnamon	5 ml
1/4 tsp	cloves	1 ml
1/4 tsp	nutmeg	1 ml

Combine the first seven ingredients in a saucepan. Cook over medium heat, stirring occasionally, until the apples are tender. Pour this mixture into a well-greased 9 x 13 inch pan.

Sift together the next four ingredients.

Cream the sugar and the shortening. Add the eggs, one at a time, beating well with a wooden spoon. Then add the milk and the sifted dry ingredients, alternately, to the creamed mixture, beginning and ending with the dry ingredients. Blend thoroughly after each addition.

Place half of this batter in a separate bowl. Blend in the last five ingredients, and then spoon the light and dark mixtures alternately over the apples.

Bake in a preheated 350°F oven for about 50 minutes, then cool in the pan. Invert onto a serving plate.

This is delicious served warm with whipped cream, which was plentiful on our farm in the 1930s. If you prefer to serve it with ice cream now, you can be forgiven. This makes a big pan, so I often divide it when it is cooked and cooled, and freeze one half for use later.

January

1 _____

_____

2 _____

_____

3 _____

_____

4 _____

_____

5 _____

_____

6 _____

_____

7 _____

_____

8 _____

_____

9 _____

_____

10 _____

_____

January

11 _____

_____

12 _____

_____

13 _____

_____

14 _____

_____

15 _____

_____

16 _____

_____

17 _____

_____

18 _____

_____

19 _____

_____

20 _____

_____

JANUARY

21 _____

_____

22 _____

_____

23 _____

_____

24 _____

_____

25 _____

_____

26 _____

_____

27 _____

_____

28 _____

_____

29 _____

_____

30 _____

_____

31 _____

_____

Table Talk

*M*other stood at the kitchen table after supper, patiently waiting for Audrey to wipe off the red-checkered oilcloth. After making sure that every last crumb and drop of gravy was gone, Audrey would dry the table thoroughly with a tea towel made from a bleached flour bag.

The kitchen table was the centre of activity every night after supper. Constructed of long wide pine boards, it seated five children and Mother and Father, with space to spare. And around it every night, I would colour the pictures that came in both the *Ottawa Farm Journal* and the *Family Herald and Weekly Star*, spreading out the job over several evenings, so that by the time I was finished, new editions of the newspapers would be in our mailbox.

Everett, Emerson and Earl played cards. Snap was a favourite, but sometimes the game got so rowdy that Mother would order them to either put the cards away or get to bed. Earl had his own deck of cards. He bought them at the five-and-dime store in Renfrew for ten cents, and he wouldn't let anyone touch them. One of his favourite pastimes was building houses with his cards, propping them against each other carefully, sometimes getting three or four cards high. But too often when that happened, Emerson would "accidentally" bump into the table, and the whole house of cards would collapse.

Emerson had his drawings to work on. With money from the sugar bowl, Mother managed to buy him big sheets of art paper at Ritza's Drugstore often enough to keep him happy. Emerson would draw buildings so strange we all thought he was going to grow up to be a bubble off plumb. "Imagine," Audrey would say, keeping her voice low so Emerson wouldn't hear her, "big buildings with glass sides. And who ever heard of elevators going up on the outside of a building? Poor Emerson. I wonder what's going to happen to him when he grows up, and discovers no one builds buildings with glass walls and outside elevators." But Emerson continued to draw his outlandish buildings at the kitchen table at night, and he kept his papers under his bed for safekeeping.

Everett was content to sit and read his library book. Over the table, hanging from the ceiling, was the Coleman lamp, much brighter than the one that burned coal oil. Through plain brute force, Mother was able to get five children library cards from the Renfrew Library, even though the librarian was dead set against country children taking books all the way out to Northcote!

The oldest of the brothers, Everett was expected to carry most of the load at chore time, and like Father, he would be dead tired by the time the supper was cleared away and the kitchen table wiped clean. He sat with his arms circling the book, and I would watch, mesmerized, as his eyes would start to droop. Soon his head would snap up and down as if he was bobbing for apples, and finally, sleep would overcome him, and his head would fall down into the circle of his arms, his face resting on the pages of his book.

My sister Audrey always sat at one end of the table with her embroidery work in a basket in front of her. Under Mother's guidance, she learned to do cross-stitching and French knots, and well-bleached flour bags were turned into pillowcases and tea towels, which came out of the drawer in the back-to-the-wall cupboard if we had company. Some of Audrey's tea towels and pillowcases were packed in an old tin trunk at the foot of our bed. This, Audrey called her "hope chest." When she told me what a hope chest was, I wondered if she would ever get to use the treasured items it held, because she was ten years older than I was, and didn't even have a boyfriend!

The other end of the table was always reserved for Mother. This is where she worked on her beloved scrapbooks and diaries. They too were kept in the bottom part of the back-to-the-wall cupboard. The scrapbooks were full of clippings from the *Philadelphia Enquirer* which she had brought in on special order to Ritza's Drugstore. Every scrap of New York City news was cut out and pasted into her books. When a book was too full to close properly, she would start on another. The rough-paper books cost a whole ten cents! So every square inch was covered...and many pieces were folded over to be made fit onto a page.

We children were allowed to look at Mother's scrapbooks whenever we wanted. Not so her diaries! Mother rarely wrote in her diaries before we went to bed. It was something she did privately when no one was around. After we had climbed the stairs, our prayers were said around her knee and we were tucked into bed, we could hear Mother bring down the Coleman lamp on its chains, and turn it off. She would then move the coal-oil lamp to her end of the old pine table and write in the dimness of the kitchen. We knew she wrote about her hopes and her dreams, and her memories of her life in New York City before she moved to the backwoods of Renfrew County. It would be many years later before we would learn of the heartache and the sadness that filled the pages of her diaries.

Father was the only one who didn't sit at the table in the evening. He preferred the rocking chair, brought up close to the Findlay Oval on a cold winter night, or pushed to an open window to catch whatever breeze there might be after the sun went down on a warm summer evening and the heat of the day had filled the old log house. With his pipe smouldering, and resting on his chest, and his stockinged feet on the seat of another chair, Father would wile away the evening, usually falling sound asleep, only to be awakened by Mother when it was time to go to bed.

So many years later, I can still see that kitchen with its old pine table, chairs at each end and a bench on either side, and I marvel at the contentment I felt. It was a time in my young life when talk of the Depression belonged to Mother and Father only, and not to a six-year-old girl whose only concern at night was trying to keep awake at that old pine table, so that she wouldn't be sent to bed before her sister and brothers.

A Casserole for Father

I can't recall Mother ever buying ground meat from the butcher shop in Renfrew. After all, our smokehouse was full of roasts, chops and hanging sausages, so there was no need to buy what we already had on hand. So when Mother wanted to make a supper dish from ground meat, she simply went to the smokehouse, took down a piece of beef, and put it through the hand-turned meat grinder that she attached to the side of the kitchen table. I hated to turn the handle of the grinder... hearing the sound of the meat being squished and sometimes seeing the blood run into the bowl. I preferred to see it when it was a finished dish for our supper.

This recipe is one of my favourites, and I have adjusted it slightly, since a couple of the items were simply not available to us back in those Depression years. Mother, of course, had our own tomatoes canned and in sealers, as buying canned tomatoes was considered extravagant in the extreme.

I can't remember that there was any such thing as a casserole dish back then. Mother used granite roasters, and our pots, of course, could go right into the oven. Perhaps the reason there were no casserole dishes in our house, was that Father didn't consider it to be a proper supper without meat, potatoes, at least two vegetables and a bowl of cabbage salad. But he did tolerate this oven dish quite happily.

Oven Dish, Plain and Simple

2 lbs	ground meat	1 kg
2 tbsp	olive oil	30 ml
1 clove	garlic	1
1	bay leaf, crumbled	1
1 tsp	ground sage	5 ml
4 cups	potatoes, thinly sliced	1 litre
1 cup	onions, thinly sliced	250 ml
28 oz can	tomatoes	796 ml
3/4 tsp	salt	3 ml

Brown the meat well in the olive oil, adding the garlic, bay leaf and sage.

Remove the meat mixture to another dish, and in the same pan, brown the potatoes, stirring often so they don't stick to the pan. (We like our potatoes crisp, so we cook them a bit longer than necessary, but do not overcook, as they will finish cooking in the baking dish.)

To the browned potatoes, add the sliced onions, salt and pepper. Cook a couple of minutes longer.

In a casserole, alternate layers of meat, potatoes and tomatoes, finishing with the potatoes and tomatoes on top. Cover and bake at 375°F for about an hour, or until the potatoes are really tender.

FEBRUARY

1 _____

_____

2 _____

_____

3 _____

_____

4 _____

_____

5 _____

_____

6 _____

_____

7 _____

_____

8 _____

_____

9 _____

_____

10 _____

_____

FEBRUARY

11 _____

_____

12 _____

_____

13 _____

_____

14 _____

_____

15 _____

_____

16 _____

_____

17 _____

_____

18 _____

_____

19 _____

_____

20 _____

_____

FEBRUARY

21 _____

_____

22 _____

_____

23 _____

_____

24 _____

_____

25 _____

_____

26 _____

_____

27 _____

_____

28 _____

_____

29 _____

_____

Two Mile and Three Mile Herman

*M*iss Crosby spun around from the blackboard as if she was on a pivot. She pointed a long, bony finger down in the general direction of Two Mile Herman. "I heard that, Herman," she bellowed. Two Mile sat there looking like an angel. "Please, miss, I didn't say nuthin'." Miss Crosby then set her sights on Cecil who sat right across from Two Mile. "All right, Cecil. What have you to say that is so important?" Cecil looked as dumbfounded as Two Mile. "Well, somebody said 'phooey'... now, who was it?"

In the Northcote School, there were two Hermans with the same last name, and to distinguish between them, we called them by the distance they lived from the schoolhouse. So we had Two Mile and Three Mile Herman. And they were as different as night and day.

Two Mile, like Cecil, was always in hot water. Three Mile was quiet, did everything he was told, wouldn't dream of misbehaving in school, did his homework diligently, kept neat scribblers, and lived in constant dread that someone would think he was related to Two Mile, which he wasn't, even though they shared the same name.

Miss Crosby started down the middle of the classroom with her thick ruler in hand, rubbing it as if she was just itching to use it on someone's head.

"No one goes out for recess until the culprit owns up to that outburst," she stated. We all looked up at the old C.P.R. clock at the front of the room. Recess was minutes away.

Miss Crosby's threats were never taken lightly. If she said there would be no recess, she meant it. We all glared at Two Mile. He sat stone-faced and still. Right behind him, Three Mile sat with his head down and his eyes fixed on his scribbler, diligently doing his arithmetic and trying his best not to be brought into the tug-of-war between the two troublemakers and Miss Crosby.

"Well?" Miss Crosby was between Cecil and Two Mile, her ruler poised for action. The two boys said nothing, although they had the common sense to sit up straight in their seats with their feet planted firmly on the floor, just the way Miss Crosby liked to see them. "Get to work, all of you," she ordered. There was no doubt about it; we were all going to pay for the outburst. Back then, that was the way the teacher meted out justice. Unless someone owned up to the deed, everyone suffered.

With our heads bent over our scribblers, we tried to glare at Cecil and Two Mile Herman without being caught. The clock passed the time for recess. We wouldn't be able to leave our desks until it was time to eat our lunches. I wondered if Miss Crosby would be mean enough to make us sit in our seats all through the noon hour too. She never took her eyes off Two Mile and Cecil. They never took their eyes off their scribblers.

Just when the clock was about to strike twelve, Three Mile Herman put up his hand. Miss Crosby, who thought the young lad could do no wrong, came down to his desk and asked him what he wanted. "Please, miss…it was me who said 'phooey.' I made a mistake in my scribbler and when I erased it, it made a hole in my page, and I just hate that." Great fat tears started to roll down his cheeks. I was sure Miss Crosby would go back up to the blackboard to get the pointer to use on Three Mile, but instead, she patted him on his heaving shoulder and returned to her desk.

She got into what we called (behind her back, of course) her praying mantis position. "Now, I hope you have all learned something from this. I am very proud of Herman. What he has just done has taken courage, and there is a lesson in this for all of you. Now, go and get your lunches from the table at the back."

My friend Joyce and I headed for the yard with our lunch boxes, wondering what the lesson was that Miss Crosby said we had just learned. Cecil and Two Mile Herman weren't at all satisfied that justice had been done. But Miss Crosby knew those two well, and she warned them if they said one word to Herman they would pay dearly for the deed.

Three Mile Herman ate his lunch by himself way over in a corner of the schoolyard. Two Mile and Cecil never said a word to him, but they glared at him as if he had committed the most serious of offences. And they should have left well enough alone, but when Miss Crosby came out on the step with the brass bell to announce that lunchtime was over, Cecil, in a voice that would have melted butter, asked her, "Please, miss, when can Herman and me talk to Herman again?"

Miss Crosby stopped with her arm halfway up in the air, the clanger coming to a stop with a loud gong. "You see, miss, Two Mile and me want to tell him something important."

38

Miss Crosby eyed Cecil with suspicion. "You can tell me what it is you want to say to him."

Cecil shifted his weight from one foot to the other. "Herman and me would just like to tell him that the next time he says "phooey" in school, we would appreciate it if he would stand up and say it real loud so you'll know it wasn't us."

Saturday Night Treats

These wonderful squares were a special treat in the 1930s. We didn't have them too often, because Mother had to buy coconut for them, which put a dent in her egg money. They *were* made regularly, though, for our Saturday night house parties, when an evening of Euchre or Five Hundred with our neighbours would be capped off with a spread of thick sandwiches of egg salad or cold sliced roast pork, and assorted sweets. These squares went particularly well with the green tea that Mother brewed and kept warm in the white granite pot on the cookstove.

Raspberry Squares

3/4 cup	raspberry jam	175 ml
1/2 cup	shortening	125 ml
1/2 cup	sugar	125 ml
2	egg yolks, beaten	2
1 cup	flour	250 ml
1/4 tsp	salt	1 ml

2	egg whites	2
1/2 cup	white sugar	125 ml
1 tsp	vanilla	5 ml
1/8 tsp	cream of tartar	1/2 ml
1 1/2 cups	coconut	375 ml

Cream the shortening and the sugar, then add the beaten egg yolks. Gradually blend in the flour and salt until a smooth paste forms.

Press this mixture into a 9 x 9 inch cake pan and bake in a moderate oven (350°F) for 15 minutes. Do not overcook.

Remove from the oven and spread with the jam. Whip the egg whites to a stiff meringue made with the sugar, vanilla and cream of tartar, and then fold in the coconut. Spread over the jam.

Return to the oven and bake about 25 minutes more, or until the top is golden, but not brown. Cut into squares while still warm.

MARCH

1 _____
_____
2 _____
_____
3 _____
_____
4 _____
_____
5 _____
_____
6 _____
_____
7 _____
_____
8 _____
_____
9 _____
_____
10 _____
_____

MARCH

11 _____

_____

12 _____

_____

13 _____

_____

14 _____

_____

15 _____

_____

16 _____

_____

17 _____

_____

18 _____

_____

19 _____

_____

20 _____

_____

MARCH

21 _____

_____

22 _____

_____

23 _____

_____

24 _____

_____

25 _____

_____

26 _____

_____

27 _____

_____

28 _____

_____

29 _____

_____

30 _____

_____

31 _____

_____

Lessons Learned at the Clothesline

$\mathcal{M}$other believed that every chore brought with it a lesson. A lesson that we could take into adulthood, making us more efficient and productive citizens. As children, we made long lists of daily chores, and something as simple as a reminder to brush our teeth, or as tiresome as making our daily entry into our diary, must first appear on our daily list. Making lists would give us direction, just as writing in our diaries would not only remind us of past mistakes but instill in us a love of record keeping. I regret to say, I was the only one of five children who went on to keep meticulous diaries, a habit I have kept to this day.

Another one of Mother's convictions was that if you learned organization at a young age, then organizational ability was yours for life. This belief was never more obvious than in our regular trips to the clothesline. Mother had a certain way of dealing with the wet clothes, and it all had to do with organization.

As they came out of the wringer, the items were put in a big oval basket with handles as big as coat hangers at each end. But to Mother, how the clothes were put into the basket was of utmost importance. All the underwear had to be piled in one corner, father's work shirts in another, socks in still another. So that we ended up with these little piles of clothes, all very separate, in the basket.

And Mother wasn't above inspecting the basket either! If she found an undershirt on top of the pillowcases, my sister Audrey and I were made to unpack the whole basket and sort all over again. So we learned at an early age that we were better off to do it right the first time...another lesson Mother was quick to point out.

This concern for like clothes in like piles, continued out at the clothes-line. Audrey and I were expected to hang the clothes every Monday morning before we went to school. Not only did we have to hang things in their respective categories, we also had to put them on the line in colour matches. All the white shirts together, all the white tea towels together, and heaven forbid that we would ever hang a tea towel next to a work sock! Audrey used to say that Mother wanted the washing to look just as nice on the line as it did on our backs.

Our clothesline stretched from the summer kitchen to the smoke house, and it caught the full force of the north wind. Even on the mildest day, when there was scarcely a breath of air, there always seemed to be a slight wind off the West Hill that sent the clothes flapping on the line. A clothesline on pulleys was only a dream of Mother's, and one she was sure would never come her way as long as we struggled to sur-vive during the Depression. After all, pulleys cost money!

Father had fashioned a long pole with a groove in one end, and this we would jab into the ground at the centre of the line, work the line into the groove, and hoist the clothes as high as we could so that none would drag on the ground. This pole had to be exactly in the centre of the line.

When we were finished, Mother would stand at the back door and inspect our work. If there was a towel out of place, or a pillow slip had been hung away from the sheets, we would be sent out to make a change before we got her approval.

There was no such thing as negotiation in those days. You did exactly as you were told. But Audrey, being the older of the two of us, one day questioned Mother about the uselessness of being so fussy about hanging out the washing. What the query got her was a long dissertation on discipline and organization. Mother always sat us down in front of her when she was giving us one of her lectures—a lesson itself that was to hold us in good stead for the rest of our lives, especially Audrey, who went on to raise 17 children.

In later years, we often talked about Mother's insistence that the clothes be hung out just so on the clothesline. We'd chuckle and laugh about it, but today I have to admit that something rankles me if I see an undershirt hanging next to the tea towels...

Everything But the Kitchen Sink

It seems to me now that the soup pot was never off the back of the stove. Leftovers, added vegetables, heels of roast beef, and anything else Mother thought would make a hearty soup, went into the pot. It was the kind of soup that stuck to the ribs and was always served at dinner (which in those days was the noon meal; supper was at night). The recipe I am giving you this month is hearty too, but it has been updated somewhat to fit today's tastes. It is a great soup to make ahead, and will keep for several days in the fridge, or can be frozen. This recipe makes at least 8 generous servings.

Ham and Potato Soup

2 tbsp	olive oil	30 ml
I	ham steak	I
	or about a pound (500 gm) of	
	leftover roasted ham, cut into cubes	
I	large sweet onion, cut into chunks	
3	large stalks of celery, cut into one-inch (2.5 cm) pieces	3

1/2 tsp	salt	2 ml
1/2 tsp	dried thyme	2 ml
1/2 tsp	caraway seeds	2 ml
1/2 tsp	pepper	2 ml
3–4	large potatoes, peeled and cut into cubes	3–4
5–6	carrots, cut into rounds	5–6
4	10-oz (284 ml) cans low-sodium chicken broth	4
1 pkg	frozen broccoli florets (thawed)	1 pkg
1 1/2 cups	half-and-half cream	375 ml

In a large pot, heat the oil, and then add the ham, browning it slightly. Do not let it burn. Remove the ham to another dish.

In the same pot, combine the onion, celery, salt, thyme, caraway seeds and pepper. Cook just until the vegetables are softened, 4 to 5 minutes.

Add the potatoes and carrots and the broth. Cook until the potatoes and carrots are fork-tender. This takes about 20 to 30 minutes.

Take 2 cups (500 ml) of the soup from the pot and purée it in a blender until smooth. Add the puréed soup and ham pieces to the soup pot. (Note: Mixture can be frozen at this point. When thawing for later use, let it thaw completely and then boil gently for 2 to 3 minutes; reduce the heat to medium.)

Rinse the broccoli, and break up into smaller pieces. Stir into the soup with the cream and reheat through for about 5 minutes. Do not boil.

April

1 _____

_____

2 _____

_____

3 _____

_____

4 _____

_____

5 _____

_____

6 _____

_____

7 _____

_____

8 _____

_____

9 _____

_____

10 _____

_____

APRIL

11 _____

_____

12 _____

_____

13 _____

_____

14 _____

_____

15 _____

_____

16 _____

_____

17 _____

_____

18 _____

_____

19 _____

_____

20 _____

_____

APRIL

21 _____

_____

22 _____

_____

23 _____

_____

24 _____

_____

25 _____

_____

26 _____

_____

27 _____

_____

28 _____

_____

29 _____

_____

30 _____

_____

Weeds, Plain and Simple

Father said they were weeds, plain and simple! "Weeds, they're the curse of the land," he'd say, peering out from under his old straw hat. Dandelions were everywhere, and they grew in our front yard in great abundance, crowding out what little grass we had.

My three brothers, if they ever dared say they were bored, would be ordered by Father to each get a knife from the kitchen, get down on their knees, and dig out the dandelions, roots and all. They were tossed into a cardboard box and thrown over the fence behind the silo. The boys hated routing out dandelions with a passion, and as soon as they thought they had the upper hand on them, there they would be again, so thick it looked as though someone had thrown a yellow blanket over the grass.

"Weeds," Father would huff, kicking them with the toe of his boot on passing. I didn't think they were weeds at all. Weeds to me were the this-tles that stung our bare feet when we walked on the grass, and the tall stalks that grew along the lane going out to the Northcote Side Road.

No, to me, dandelions in bloom were as soft as velvet—like little silk cushions when I held them in my hand. I would pick them, with their short stems, and put them in a little glass of water to take up to the washstand in my bedroom. Audrey, who shared the room with me, thought I was crazy. "No one picks dandelions for flowers," she'd say, making a face to show her disgust.

Mother knew they were weeds too. But she also knew they could be put to good use. Mrs. Beam, that wonderful German neighbour who did everything from delivering babies to curing whooping cough, told Mother about using dandelions as a vegetable. Father thought Mother had taken leave of her senses the first time she brought a steaming bowl of dandelions to the supper table. "Weeds," he scoffed. "Just plain weeds." Mother had cooked only the tender green leaves, barely boiling them so they stayed firm. She then laced them with butter and salt and pepper.

He looked at the bowl for a long time, and finally, seeing nothing else on his plate to accompany the usual meat and potatoes, he scraped up a few leaves with his fork and popped them into his mouth in much the same way as he would a dose of castor oil. He ran them around in his mouth, and I never took my eyes off him. I was sure he was going to rush over to the Findlay Oval, take off the lid, and spit the whole lot into the firebox.

Mother was watching him also out of the corner of her eye. He reached over and brought the bowl closer to his plate and dug out a heaping spoonful. I could hear mother making "humph" sounds from her place at the stove. Father heard her too. "Well, what do you expect a man to do when there's nothing else on the table? Can't work all day in the fields and not eat," Father said, sopping up the last of the butter on his plate with a crust of bread.

54

Interestingly, Father didn't call dandelions "weeds" late in the summer when he gathered them in a bushel basket to make his usual batch of dandelion wine. I no longer remember the process, but I do remember Uncle Herby, who worked for Bronfman Distilleries in Montreal, telling Father that his dandelion wine was the best he ever tasted, and that he thought Father could make a fortune if he sold it. Mother reminded him it was against the law to sell homebrew, which soon settled that idea.

I know now, so many years later, that I got more pleasure from the dandelions than anyone else. I would pick them carefully, making sure I kept the stalks intact, and then I would split the ends and they would curl down in perfect little tendrils. I would tuck them into my long red ringlets, or put them through a buttonhole in my blouse. Sometimes I would just daydream, sitting in the old swing in the grape arbour and rolling down the stems of freshly picked dandelions, until I had a dozen or so laid out in my lap, like precious jewels.

Our Smokehouse Bounty

Our smokehouse always had an ample supple of pork roasts, and Mother would take a roast off a hook and slice between the bones to create pork chops, which everyone in the family thought a great treat. She made her own sweet-and-sour sauce with vinegar, brown sugar and honey, but today we have the convenient option of buying a variety of barbecue sauces in a bottle.

Pork Chops with Barbecue Sauce

pork chops (any number)
flour
salt and pepper
olive oil
barbecue sauce

Wipe the pork chops with a damp cloth, and then dredge both sides with flour. Season sparingly with salt and pepper.

Sear chops in olive oil in a skillet until nicely browned on both sides. Spread a tablespoon (15 ml) of barbecue sauce on each chop. Reduce the heat, cover, and cook slowly for about 10 minutes.

Turn the chops and place 1 tablespoon (15 ml) barbecue sauce on this side. Cover again and cook on low heat until tender, about 40 minutes. Check occasionally to ensure that there is enough moisture to keep the chops tender; if not, add a bit more sauce.

When ready to serve, heat a small amount of extra barbecue sauce to serve as a side with the chops. This dish is especially good served with creamy mashed potatoes.

MAY

1 _____

_____

2 _____

_____

3 _____

_____

4 _____

_____

5 _____

_____

6 _____

_____

7 _____

_____

8 _____

_____

9 _____

_____

10 _____

_____

MAY

11 _____

_____

12 _____

_____

13 _____

_____

14 _____

_____

15 _____

_____

16 _____

_____

17 _____

_____

18 _____

_____

19 _____

_____

20 _____

_____

MAY

21 _____

_____

22 _____

_____

23 _____

_____

24 _____

_____

25 _____

_____

26 _____

_____

27 _____

_____

28 _____

_____

29 _____

_____

30 _____

_____

31 _____

_____

The Raft

Father said the best wood to use in making a raft was cedar. It was light and would float better than any other wood we had on the farm...and goodness knows we had lots of cedar!

Emerson got the idea of a raft after reading a book borrowed from the Renfrew Library, and it didn't take much persuasion to get Everett and Earl involved in the project too. But of course, Emerson had to draw up the plans first.

Father said there was no need for plans. You simply put spikes through a few planks to secure them to the cedar logs and that was it. But Emerson never missed an opportunity to put his ideas to paper. He spread out two pieces of foolscap and went to work at the kitchen table.

Hours later, when it was time to go to bed, Emerson still hadn't finished his plans. I looked over his shoulder, and thought what he had drawn looked as though it could sail the Atlantic. Everett said, ready or not, they were starting to put the raft together in the morning.

Emerson took his plans, which had grown from two sheets of foolscap to about ten, and shoved them under his bed where he kept his other drawings of buildings made of glass, with elevators going up the outside walls. We kids thought he was strange. Mother thought he was a genius.

The next day, as soon as the boys finished their chores, Emerson was back at the kitchen table with his papers. Everett and Earl were cutting cedar logs and hauling boards from a stack at the back of the silo. Using the axe, they pointed one end of each log. Everett said that would make the raft slip through the water more easily. By afternoon, the raft was finished, and Emerson was still at the kitchen table. Father helped put a toggle on the front end of the raft, and then he harnessed up King, who would drag the raft down to the Bonnechere.

Audrey, the motherly type, said she felt badly that Emerson wasn't there to see it being put in the water. Everett said it was his own fault. "Him and his high falootin' ideas," he said.

Father stopped King halfway down the hill that led to the field we would have to cross to get to the river. "Mary, run up to the house and get Emerson."

Everett and Earl, not too pleased, sat down on the raft while I tore up the West Hill to fetch Emerson. A pile of scrunched-up paper was beside him on the kitchen table. "Come on, Emerson, the raft is going into the water," I yelled from the back door.

Emerson ran from the table like someone possessed. He told me to rush down to Father and tell him to wait, he'd be there as soon as he collected something from the woodshed. We both arrived at the raft at the same time, and in his hand, Emerson had an old Watkins vanilla bottle filled with water. The procession continued.

"Can't put a raft in the Bonnechere without a proper launching," he said, his face beet-red from running all the way there. "And just what are you planning on doing with that bottle of water?" Father asked, as if he didn't know.

"It has to have a name. Now, let's see, what about calling it *The Northcote Schooner*? Everett, you say the name, and I'll break the bottle over the logs at the back."

Father said there would be no bottle broken over the logs on the raft and that was final. Everett and Earl wanted to know how come Emerson got involved in the first place, when he hadn't lifted a finger to build the thing. Everett gave Emerson a poke, and Earl, the smallest of the three brothers, had no intention of getting physical, but yelled, "Yeah, Emerson, how come?"

Father settled the argument by warning them if the squabbling didn't stop, the raft could go back up the West Hill and stay there till hell froze over.

That settled everyone down and the procession began again, with King dragging the raft to the river. Since Father wouldn't hear of Emerson breaking the bottle on the butt end of a log in the raft, Emerson said he'd settle for just pouring the water over the raft and saying a few appropriate words.

Whenever we buried a bird, a frog, or any other creature that had expired on the farm, Emerson always had to say a few words. It appeared to me that the launching of this raft was taking on the same tone as a burial.

Emerson asked Father, Everett and Earl to take off their straw hats. Father never moved a muscle, but Everett and Earl, itching to get their raft in the water, took off their hats and held them close to their chests.

I have no idea of all that Emerson said, but he ended up by declaring in a solemn voice, "In the name of the King, I name thee *The Northcote Schooner.*" With that, he turned the bottle upside down and the water poured over the last six inches of the raft.

I asked my older and much wiser sister Audrey what the King had to do with it. With a heavy sigh, she replied, "Like Emerson, not much."

Chickens Aplenty

Chicken certainly wasn't a treat when I was growing up in those Depression years. It found its way to our table often, because chickens were plentiful. We had chicken and dumplings almost every Sunday. Mother could put it on to simmer before we went to church. Often, when we got home, a carload of relatives would have descended on the farm from the city, and one of my brothers would be dispatched to bring in another chicken or two to add to the pot.

Mother made big fat dumplings that never failed to turn out fluffy and delicious. The liquid in the pot would be turned into a rich gravy, and I can remember our Ottawa relatives remarking that by some miracle the Depression had bypassed us out on that Renfrew County farm, so laden was our Sunday table.

The recipe that follows is a new find, however, one that has nothing to do with those Depression dinners of long ago. It has become a family favourite of ours now, so many years later.

Recipe, next page

Baked Honey Mustard Chicken

1/3 cup	prepared mustard	75 ml
1/3 cup	honey	75 ml
2 tbsp	crushed dill (use fresh dill, if available)	30 ml
2 tsp	freshly ground orange peel	10 ml
1	chicken quartered	1
	If you prefer, you can use boneless, skinless chicken breasts,	
	but the bone-in pieces enhance the flavour of this recipe.	

Make the sauce ahead of time by combining the mustard and honey in a small bowl, then stirring in the dill and orange peel. Set aside until the chicken is ready to be baked.

Preheat the oven to 400°F. Line a baking sheet with foil. Spray with Pam, or brush lightly with olive oil. Place chicken skin side down if you are using pieces, and brush the chicken thoroughly with the honey mustard sauce.

Partway through cooking, turn the chicken over, and again brush well with the sauce. Use up all the sauce, brushing both sides until it is all gone. Bake until the chicken shows juices running clear when pierced with a fork. This takes about 45 minutes—or 30 minutes for boneless, skinless breasts.

JUNE

1 _____

_____

2 _____

_____

3 _____

_____

4 _____

_____

5 _____

_____

6 _____

_____

7 _____

_____

8 _____

_____

9 _____

_____

10 _____

_____

JUNE

11 _____

_____

12 _____

_____

13 _____

_____

14 _____

_____

15 _____

_____

16 _____

_____

17 _____

_____

18 _____

_____

19 _____

_____

20 _____

_____

JUNE

21 _____

_____

22 _____

_____

23 _____

_____

24 _____

_____

25 _____

_____

26 _____

_____

27 _____

_____

28 _____

_____

29 _____

_____

30 _____

_____

Egg Money

Mrs. Beam seemed to know everything that was going on at Northcote, and Mother relied on her to help her ease into being a farmer's wife and get to know the community. After living for eighteen years in New York City before moving to the backwoods of Renfrew County, there was much Mother didn't know about country living.

It was Mrs. Beam who showed Mother how to can beans with brine so they would last all winter, and it was Mrs. Beam who everyone on the entire Northcote Side Road called on if there was sickness in the house, or it was time to deliver a baby.

It was one of those hot summer days when the sun beat down on the old log house, and Mother had covered the windows with blankets to keep out the heat. The only room where you could see your hand in front of you was the summer kitchen, and that's where Mother and Mrs. Beam were sitting that day, drinking cold tea and lamenting the sad state of the country where, as Mrs. Beam said, "nickels were as scarce as hen's teeth."

"I don't know what I would do without my egg money," said Mrs. Beam. Mother came back with, "Well, the money I get from selling eggs in Renfrew doesn't amount to much."

Mrs. Beam paused for a moment and then explained that the money wasn't really just egg money. It was every penny of money she made, not only from selling eggs but from selling anything else that wasn't nailed down. And she threw back her head and laughed.

Mother interest was immediate. She asked her neighbour to explain further. "Well," said Mrs. Beam, her eyes scrunched tight, as if she were telling some deep secret, "every farm woman I know has what we call egg money. Now, it doesn't necessarily mean it comes just from eggs. You know those socks I knit? Well, the money I get from every pair I sell goes into the bowl where I keep my egg money," and she took on a smug look as if she had just announced that she had invented the telephone. "And no one touches that money. It's mine to do with as I please." She said if she wanted new print for a housedress, or wanted to have her hair cut by Mrs. Ducharme in Renfrew, she used the money from her bowl.

Well, Mother had never heard of egg money coming from anything other than the sale of eggs. But as soon as Mrs. Beam went out to the buggy, Mother went to the back-to-the-wall cupboard, and took down the big blue sugar bowl. We never used it for sugar, because it had a lid that had to be taken off every time it was used, which Father said was just a plain nuisance.

At supper that night, Mother announced that no one was to touch the blue sugar bowl but her, and she described to all of us the sugar bowl's newly expanded role. "Maybe I can save enough to go back to visit Rosie in New York," she said, looking off into space to the farthest corner of the kitchen. And she opened the glass door of the cupboard, and put the sugar bowl up on the top shelf. I was sure Father snorted, but he said nothing. Mother wrote to Rosie and told her all about her egg money and the blue sugar bowl, and said she looked forward to the day she would have enough money saved to go back to New York for a visit.

Well, that sugar bowl became just as important to Mother as the linen tablecloth she brought to the farm. Every Saturday, after her trip into Renfrew for supplies, Mother emptied her purse, and the few pennies she had left over, went into the sugar bowl.

And her wares expanded beyond just eggs. She made homemade soap and sticky buns, and began selling vegetables and apples in the fall. Every spare penny went into the blue sugar bowl.

As the Depression ground on, with less and less money to be had, and it hardly paid to feed the livestock over the winter, Mother and Father talked in whispers about the sad state of the economy. And even though there was little money coming in, there were still bills to be met and expenses around the farm. A piece of harness had to be replaced; the inner tubes on the old Model T would not take another patch; a new plow point was needed. The only spare money was what Mother had saved in the blue sugar bowl. Her egg money. At first Father would ask to borrow a bit...maybe a dollar or two. And Mother would take the bowl down from the cupboard and count out the change he needed. There was less and less money going into the sugar bowl. And more and more being taken out.

It got to the point where Father didn't even ask Mother for a couple of dollars. He would just go to the cupboard, take down the bowl and take what he needed. Father always looked so sad when he had to go to the sugar bowl, and Mother would just let out a deep sigh and turn her head away. The visit back to New York City was never mentioned again.

Beyond Cabbage Salad

Tossed salads were unheard of when I was growing up in the Depression years. However, cabbage salad was a staple, and when the cabbages were ready to be picked from the garden, coleslaw, made with Mother's homemade salad dressing, would appear often on our supper table.

In our household, the cabbages were mainly saved for making sauerkraut—an exercise that involved the whole family. Cabbages that had been wrapped in several layers of the *Renfrew Mercury* were stored in a cool place until it came time to roll the big barrel into the kitchen, mount the slicer, get out the bag of coarse salt, and all hands got into the chore of preparing the sauerkraut. Once packed in the barrel, and salted down, the cabbage formed its own juices. The barrel would be rolled out into the cold summer kitchen, and by the time the snow covered the ground, its contents would be frozen solid. Sauerkraut was a staple back then, and when Father added his German touch to a sauerkraut dish, it was a treat we all enjoyed.

As the years rolled by, other dishes took the place of coleslaw and sauerkraut. I discovered the following wonderful salad not long after I was married. A tasty dish for company that serves at least 8 people.

Bean and Pasta Delight

2–3 cups	cooked macaroni	500–750 ml
I tin	each of yellow, green and red kidney beans	I tin
1/4 cup	vinegar	50 ml
1/4 cup	white sugar	50 ml
3 tbsp	olive oil	45 ml
I cup	chopped celery	250 ml
4	eggs, hard-boiled and chilled, chopped coarsely	4
1/2– 2/3 cup	creamy French dressing	125–150 ml
1/4 cup	sweet pickle relish	50 ml
I /2 tsp	salt	2 ml
	a few drops hot pepper sauce (optional)	
	dash of freshly ground pepper	

In a large glass bowl, combine the macaroni, beans, vinegar, sugar and oil. Mix thoroughly but gently, so as not to break down the beans. Taste, and add vinegar if more "tart" taste is needed, or more sugar if you want a sweeter taste. Add celery and eggs. Stir just to mix. Mix together the French dressing, relish, pepper sauce, salt and pepper. Pour over the macaroni mixture, and toss lightly. This dish can be made a couple of hours before you want to serve it, because it should be thoroughly chilled at least an hour. I hard-boil and slice two extra eggs, to garnish the top of the salad just before serving.

JULY

1 _____

_____

2 _____

_____

3 _____

_____

4 _____

_____

5 _____

_____

6 _____

_____

7 _____

_____

8 _____

_____

9 _____

_____

10 _____

_____

July

11 _____

_____

12 _____

_____

13 _____

_____

14 _____

_____

15 _____

_____

16 _____

_____

17 _____

_____

18 _____

_____

19 _____

_____

20 _____

_____

JULY

21 _____

_____

22 _____

_____

23 _____

_____

24 _____

_____

25 _____

_____

26 _____

_____

27 _____

_____

28 _____

_____

29 _____

_____

30 _____

_____

31 _____

_____

The Overnight Visitor

*M*arguerite was hard to like. I suppose now that it was part envy, but she was my worst enemy at the Northcote School. First of all, she was an only child, which put her a cut above everyone else since most families out where we lived had at least four or five children, and a few had close to a dozen children. Small families were as scarce as hen's teeth. So here was Marguerite—an only child, whose doting parents gave her just about anything she wanted. She was the only one in the entire school who had black patent leather Mary Janes and pure white stockings. Her hair ribbons were wide, made of satin, and she had one to match every dress she ever wore.

And if she didn't get her way, she ran to Miss Crosby and was known to tell a barefaced lie to win her sympathy. She always had something special in her lunch, like fresh fruit that didn't grow on a tree in her backyard, and store-bought meat, a luxury we could only dream about.

So Marguerite and I certainly couldn't be considered friends. Only when there was no one else to play with, did she condescend to come to my house, and all the time she was there, she continually talked about all the other places she had been invited to, which I also knew to be far from the truth.

For reasons that escape me today, Marguerite's mother had asked if her daughter could spend the night at our house. No matter the reason, the girl who caused me such anguish at the Northcote School was to stay over. School had yet to start for the new year, and that August was hot and humid. The evening Marguerite arrived with her leather suitcase, the upstairs bedrooms were like the inside of an oven. All day the sun had pounded down on the tarpaper roof, and there wasn't a breath of air anywhere.

My brothers had little use for Marguerite, but they had been warned by Mother that they were to show the same respect she would expect them to give to any visitor who came to spend the night. Supper passed uneventfully, in spite of the fact Marguerite made it known that at her house they always had a linen tablecloth with napkins to match. Well, the only time our best tablecloth came out was at Christmas or when some notable came for a meal, and Marguerite certainly wasn't a notable!

She refused to play cards after supper, and said singsongs (Mother had long ago mastered the harmonica and evenings often ended with a family singsong) were for Salvation Army bands on a street corner in Renfrew.

Suffice it to say that the whole evening got off to a bad start. When it came time to go to bed, we climbed the stairs, with Marguerite lugging her genuine leather suitcase behind her. When I stayed overnight at Joyce's or Velma's house, my nightgown was stuffed in a brown paper bag. But Marguerite's nightgown was neatly folded with a little pair of hand-knit slippers placed just so on top of it. Emerson, who had to pass through our bedroom to get to the back room where he and Everett shared a bed, said it looked like she was going on a honeymoon.

Marguerite eyed the feather ticking on the bed in dismay, declaring they used real mattresses at her house. Well, for her, it was either the feather ticking or the floor that night!

After much ado, she finally settled down, but only after she changed places with me twice. At first she wanted to be beside the wall. Then she said she wanted to be on the outside. I was worn out from the tension, and all I wanted to do was go to sleep!

Before too many minutes passed, Marguerite hissed that she had to go to the bathroom. Well, the bathroom at our house in the middle of the night was the chamber pot under the bed. My sister Audrey had to get up and light the lamp, and Marguerite was directed to the pot at the foot of the bed. "How do you use it?" she asked in a loud whisper. Well, our walls were paper-thin, and the brothers in the back bedroom could hear every word. "You sit on it, you ninny," Emerson roared.

Well, that's all it took for Marguerite to burst into tears. Audrey had to lead her downstairs, through the kitchen, and out the back door to the privy. When she returned with Marguerite, Audrey was not happy. And when Audrey wasn't happy, everyone knew it! "If you have to go again, Marguerite, you can use the chamber pot, or hang your rear end out the window." That caused the brothers to erupt into fits of laughing, and brought Mother to the bottom of the stairs. "Settle down all of you. Audrey, you're the oldest, and I expect you to keep things under control up there."

Marguerite tossed and turned, said the feathers in the ticking had shifted to one big lump, and she couldn't wait to get into her own bed at home. Well, that suited me just fine.

She finally fell asleep, but the night wasn't over by a long shot. She started to snore. At the start, it was just little whimpering puffs, and at first I thought she was crying. Then the noise turned into a sound just like air escaping from a balloon. I sat up on one elbow, and looked over at her. I could barely see her outline beside me in the dark room, but she was lying on her back, and I could tell she was asleep. Nobody else was. Emerson yelled from the back room for me to put a pillow over her head. Everett said to give her a good shake. Earl, who could sleep through anything, took his pillow and headed for the cretonne couch in the kitchen. It was the longest of nights. Everyone woke up in a bad mood, including Marguerite, who vowed she never slept a wink.

Her little leather suitcase was sitting at the back door, and when her mother drove into the yard, Marguerite grabbed it by the handle and tore out to the car like someone possessed. With so little sleep, my three brothers, my sister and I were grumpy all day. That night Audrey suggested we skip the singsong. Mother said we could say our prayers to ourselves when we got into bed. She knew that even though it was still daylight in the evening in late August, we would all be heading up to bed before it got dark to catch up on the sleep we had missed the night before.

For the Love of Celery

The one time I remember Mother trying to grow celery, it turned out to be a complete disaster. Father warned her it wouldn't grow, but she longed for the crisp celery she used to buy from the street market in New York City, and she was determined she could harvest it out there in Renfrew County! I have no idea what happened to it, but it never grew higher than a couple of inches, and what did come out of the ground the crows ate up with great relish.

Buying celery was not an option back then. If you didn't grow your own vegetables, you certainly didn't go out and spend hard-earned dollars on something as frivolous as celery. Perhaps it is because it was such a luxury when I was little, that I developed a real love of celery. However, I found there were very few recipes you could use it in, other than a salad. The following recipe was a real find for me, and elegant enough to use for a special dinner party. I often double it for a crowd, but this recipe will serve 6 nicely.

Celery Extraordinaire

2 cups	celery, cut diagonally	500 ml
	and sliced to half-inch (12 mm) thickness	
1 – 8 oz can	sliced water chestnuts, drained	250 ml
1/2 cup	toasted slivered almonds	125 ml
1/4 cup	chopped pimento	50 ml
1/4 cup, plus 2 tbsp	butter	50 ml, plus 30 ml
3 tbsp	flour	45 ml
2/3 cup	half-and-half cream	150 ml
2/3 cup	chicken broth	150 ml
	Dash of salt	
3/4 cup	bread crumbs	175 ml
1/3 cup	butter melted	75 ml
1/4 cup	grated Parmesan cheese	50 ml
	dash of paprika	

Cook the celery in boiling water for about 4 minutes. Drain well. Combine the celery, chestnuts, almonds and pimento, and turn into a well-greased baking dish.

Melt the butter over very low heat, and add flour, stirring until smooth. Cook one minute, stirring constantly, and then gradually add the cream and the chicken broth. Cook, stirring constantly, until the mixture thickens and starts to bubble. Add salt to taste.

Pour the sauce over the celery mixture. Mix the bread crumbs with the melted butter and Parmesan, and sprinkle over the casserole. Sprinkle on the paprika.

Bake in a 350°F oven for about 40 minutes or until hot and bubbly.

AUGUST

1 _____

_____

2 _____

_____

3 _____

_____

4 _____

_____

5 _____

_____

6 _____

_____

7 _____

_____

8 _____

_____

9 _____

_____

10 _____

_____

AUGUST

11 _____

_____

12 _____

_____

13 _____

_____

14 _____

_____

15 _____

_____

16 _____

_____

17 _____

_____

18 _____

_____

19 _____

_____

20 _____

_____

AUGUST

21 _____

_____

22 _____

_____

23 _____

_____

24 _____

_____

25 _____

_____

26 _____

_____

27 _____

_____

28 _____

_____

29 _____

_____

30 _____

_____

31 _____

_____

Suitably Named...Piano

The only person who ever called him by his right name was Miss Crosby. She wouldn't tolerate nicknames, so we had to be very careful when we called the young lad in Senior Fourth "Piano," that she was nowhere in sight. Piano's real name was Delbern—not Delbert like the boy who came all the way from the Fifth Line—but Delbern. But the entire school called him Piano.

I had to have the reason for his nickname explained to me by my older and much wiser sister Audrey. "That's because his teeth look like piano keys," she said in a low whisper.

After Audrey's explanation, I took a much keener interest in Piano, and took every opportunity to sidle up to him and have a good look at his teeth. They were straight as a die, and when he smiled, his teeth *did* look like the keys on the piano in the United Church Sunday School hall. He wore his nickname like a badge, and seemed quite pleased that his teeth were likened to something as grand as a piano.

But Piano had a mean streak in him, and you were wise to keep on the good side of him. His favourite trick was to come up behind you when you were walking, and stick his foot between your feet. You would fall headfirst, like a stone.

Before we had a double privy, with one side for boys and the other for girls, we had only a one-holer that sat behind a cluster of bushes, well out of sight of the school. Miss Crosby preferred that we use the privy during recess or the lunch hour, so we wouldn't be constantly interrupting the class. So there was always a lineup as soon as we were excused from class, and the girls who could run the fastest got first dibs on the privy. We hardly ever saw the boys go into it, and rumour had it that they just went outside by the rink fence at the end of the schoolyard.

Like just about every other boy back then, Piano always had his pockets stuffed with "things." A slingshot hung out of his back pocket, and he could extract everything from a jackknife to a screwdriver from the front of his overalls. His pockets always bulged out, and I was reasonably sure he wasn't above cramming in a frog or a snake if the spirit moved him.

For reasons I never knew, Piano was mad at the world and, especially, the girls at the Northcote School. The day was warm for early September, and we were all anxious for recess so we could escape from the stuffy schoolroom. Although Miss Crosby expected us to leave the school in an orderly fashion, Cecil, Emerson and Piano made a beeline for the door, and were outside before most of us were out of our seats.

The senior girls were sedately walking towards the back of the yard, lining up to enter the privy. We younger ones knew we would have to wait our turn. It was Cecil who stopped the senior girls in their tracks by telling them that Piano had gone to shoo away a large garter snake he had spotted on the step going into the privy. "He'll tell us when it's safe to go there," Cecil added with an air of authority.

I was jumping from one foot to the next, wondering if I could hold out until all the girls had gone in to do what we called back then "their business." Then we saw Piano sauntering over in our direction. He had a branch in his hand, signifying that he had indeed accomplished his good deed.

Audrey and her friend Iva were the first to reach the privy, with the rest of us lined up behind them like sheep. And then we saw it. Wrapped around the privy entirely was a chain with a padlock on it, sealing the place up tighter than a clam!

Cecil, Emerson and Piano were doubled over laughing. Marguerite, who was scared of no one, raced to the school to tell Miss Crosby. We only had fifteen-minute recesses, and Miss Crosby was already on the stoop with the big brass bell. She made a dash for the privy and it didn't take a genius to figure out who was behind the deed. The three culprits were lined up at the fence with "guilty" written all over their faces.

"Unlock that chain this instant," Miss Crosby hollered. "Gee, Miss Crosby, I really would like to, but I swallowed the key," Piano answered. "Well, you better figure out a way to get it out of your stomach or you will spend the rest your life at the Northcote School sitting on the dunce's stool."

Cecil and Emerson, sure they would be in for the same fate, and short on loyalty when it came to Piano, said he didn't swallow the key at all, that it was in his back pocket. Piano glared at them, but thrust his hand into his pocket and ambled over to the chain as though he had all the time in the world. He undid the lock, and the chain fell to the ground.

Audrey went up to Miss Crosby and asked to speak to her privately. Miss Crosby listened, and then announced that since it was no fault of theirs that they couldn't get into the privy, recess would be extended for the girls. The boys would go back into the school, and they had better be quick about it.

Sitting out the rest of the day on the dunce's stool at the front of the classroom was the lesser of Piano's punishments. Every day thereafter, he was ordered to arrive at the school early in order to pour lime powder down the one-holer—a sissy job reserved for the girls of Senior Fourth.

It would be nice to say that Piano mended his ways. However, it seems to me now, so many years later, that as he got older, his pranks worsened. But time lessens the impact of Piano's deeds, and although no one would ever have fathomed it at the time, the young lad called Piano went into the ministry. And, of course, once he left the Northcote School, no one ever again referred to him as Piano. It was Delbern, and the whole community would say, "What a fine young man, that Delbern. You *know*, he's the one who became a minister."

Fall Stores

It was a poor farmer, indeed, who couldn't keep food on the table for his family. On our farm, there were always lots of vegetables; we had a couple of wild apple trees, and berries were plentiful; and the smoke-house was always full of meat. There was a big pork barrel in our kitchen, along with a smaller barrel that held pickled herring.

One of my favourite meals growing up was a wonderful baked ham dish. Sadly, I can't remember all Mother did to it to give it such a robust and delicious flavour. But I have devised my own recipe, and tried to come as close as possible to the baked ham Mother used to turn out. I often keep a ham steak on hand, and serve this for unexpected guests. It's easy to prepare, and I can have it on the table in less than an hour. This recipe allows for 4 good-sized servings.

Recipe, next page

Company Honeyed Ham

1 28 oz can	peach halves in heavy syrup	796 ml
1	fully cooked smoked ham, centre-cut slice, about 1 1/2 pounds	1
1/2 cup	orange juice	125 ml
2 tbsp	honey	30 ml
2 tsp	prepared mustard	10 ml
1/4 tsp	ground allspice	1 ml
2–3 tbsp	water	30–45 ml
1 tsp	corn starch	5 ml
	You may have to add more corn starch, depending on the consistency of the juices.	
	olive oil	

Drain the peaches, reserving 1/2 cup (125 ml) of the syrup. Grease a skillet with olive oil. Lightly brown ham on both sides, about 5 or 6 minutes.

To the ham, add the orange juice, honey, mustard, allspice and the reserved peach juice. Add the peach halves (being careful not to break them). Cook over medium heat until the peaches are heated through.

Remove ham and peaches to a serving platter, leaving the liquids in the pan. In a small bowl, stir the water and cornstarch until well blended, and stir into the hot liquid in the pan. Cook over medium heat, stirring constantly until the mixture is thickened. Let it come to a full boil, stirring, for 1 to 2 minutes.

Spoon the sauce over the ham and peaches. Keep warm in the oven, or serve immediately.

SEPTEMBER

1 _____
_____

2 _____
_____

3 _____
_____

4 _____
_____

5 _____
_____

6 _____
_____

7 _____
_____

8 _____
_____

9 _____
_____

10 _____
_____

SEPTEMBER

11 _____

_____

12 _____

_____

13 _____

_____

14 _____

_____

15 _____

_____

16 _____

_____

17 _____

_____

18 _____

_____

19 _____

_____

20 _____

_____

SEPTEMBER

21 _____

_____

22 _____

_____

23 _____

_____

24 _____

_____

25 _____

_____

26 _____

_____

27 _____

_____

28 _____

_____

29 _____

_____

30 _____

_____

Adding Space Where None Exists

If only the old log house had been larger. Mother constantly lamented that it was beyond her how anyone could have raised seven children, tended to two aging grandparents, and kept their sanity in a house meant for two people at best. But that was the house Father had grown up in, and he reminded Mother of the fact every time she complained about the size of the home that had been built a century earlier.

The kitchen was the largest room on the main floor, with a small parlour and a bedroom that Mother said looked like an afterthought. Upstairs there were only three rooms, one not much bigger than a clothes closet, and the main hall which was the room Audrey and I shared.

When the whole issue of the small house came around again, it was late fall, but it was still warm. Father said it was one of the longest Indian summers he had ever witnessed.

Early in the summer, the big cumbersome Findlay Oval cookstove had been moved from the house to the summer kitchen. That allowed the rest of the house to be as cool as possible, keeping the blasting heat from the stove confined to the little lean-to that in the wintertime held rows of wood for the stove and the sauerkraut barrel, and not much else.

It was that year, when we were enjoying the longest Indian summer Father said he could remember, that Mother said she thought with a little planning and a bit of fixing up, the summer kitchen could be kept open all winter. "Just think what a wonderful big room we would have to sit around in if we didn't put the cookstove back in the house," she remarked.

Father said it was the craziest idea he had ever heard of. He reminded her that there was nothing but plain boards for walls in the summer kitchen, the windows wouldn't close properly, and you could run a two-by-four under the door. Mother called those minor adjustments that would have to be dealt with, and announced the Findlay Oval was going to stay exactly where it had sat since April. Father, as usual, decided the best thing to do in such a situation was to let Mother learn the hard way, and the discussion was closed.

The brothers were delighted they wouldn't have to haul the big stove back into the house. It usually took the better part of a Saturday, by the time the pipes were taken down, painted and put back up in the house, and the big stove hauled inside on logs and planks. Emerson said the day would be better spent hunting rabbits.

Mother set about getting the summer kitchen ready for the onslaught of the severe winter for which Renfrew County was famous. Father just looked on, occasionally shaking his head and wondering aloud when she was going to come to her senses.

Mother nailed a rolled-up rug to the bottom of the door, and said she would defy the cold to penetrate it. She stuffed the crooked window frames with old wool socks, and ran newspapers in every crack she could find in the walls. Then she revved up the old Findlay Oval and we children admitted that the summer kitchen was just about as hot as the inside of our old log house on the coldest Ottawa Valley winter day. Mother was beaming over her success and raving about how nice it was going to be to have more living space in the house. Father could be heard muttering under his breath in German, which was the closest he ever got to swearing. He had no patience for anyone with such little respect for Renfrew County winters.

Indian summer continued on for a time, with each day getting just a tad colder, but Mother kept the Findlay Oval jumping, and the heat from the summer kitchen wafted into the kitchen, keeping the house cosy and warm. It cooled off at night, though, as the pipes that usually snaked upstairs and out through the chimney in the back bedroom were not there. When we complained, Mother said we'd get used to it. That comment earned her a raised eyebrow and a snort from Father.

By the first of November, Indian summer was just a fond memory. Winter was about to settle in. The summer kitchen was still warm, but the rest of the house was as cold as the Bonnechere River, which would soon be freezing over. But Mother still held to her idea of leaving the Findlay Oval in the summer kitchen. And then the snow came without warning, and Father said, "Right on time, like it always does." Now, we could see our breath in the upstairs bedrooms, and even the vacant kitchen was too cold to sit in on an evening. We huddled around the stove in the summer kitchen at night, the mat nailed to the back door doing little to keep out the wind. Every morning we would get up to see a little mountain of snow in front of it.

Upstairs in the morning, it was so cold that the ankles on our long underwear we had washed out the night before so they would be snug for school the next day, were frozen solid at the foot of our beds. We took to grabbing our clothes and making a beeline for the summer kitchen. And then one morning when we were all huddled around the stove, the last of the papers and socks Mother had stuffed around the windows gave one last flutter and fell to the floor, and we couldn't see the glass for the frost.

In the main kitchen, the wash basin that had been filled with fresh water the night before was a solid block of ice. Even the water in the kettle was frozen. Father said it would take until spring to thaw out the house. He had his bearskin coat on over his long underwear, and his breath curled out of his mouth like smoke from a pipe. He kept saying over and over again, "Some people just have to learn the hard way."

There was no time for frivolity that day. With mitts and hats, the boys and Father dismantled the stovepipes. There was no mention of giving them their usual coat of silver paint. Planks were laid across four logs, and the big iron stove was heaved on top. It didn't take long to roll it the few feet into the kitchen. It took longer to feel any benefit from the raging fire Father got going once the stove was put back together. By that night, the old log house was warm again, and the summer kitchen was officially closed for the winter.

Father started to say something, but Mother cut him off at the pass. "Not one word, Albert Haneman, not one word," was all she said to bring the issue to a close.

No More Bread Pudding!

Desserts were pretty simple on the farm in the 1930s. Pies and butter tarts were special treats, and nothing could beat a chocolate layer cake! (Sadly, there was also bread pudding, which I hated with a passion when it arrived at the supper table—too often.)

The recipe for this sponge cake came to me long after I was married, and the Depression years were but a memory. What I especially like about this cake is that it can be made ahead and frozen for later use. So if you are planning a luncheon, or just want to be prepared for unexpected guests, this sponge cake is ideal to have on hand.

Standby Sponge Cake

1 1/2 cups	softened butter (do not use margarine)	375 ml
2 tbsp	grated lemon rind	30 ml
1 cup	white sugar, divided	250 ml
3	large eggs	3
1 1/2 cups	sifted flour	375 ml

1/4 tsp	salt	1 ml
1/2 cup	blanched sliced almonds	125 ml
1/2 cup	candied cherries, chopped	125 ml

I sometimes use other candied fruit I happen to have in the cupboard.
If you like lots of fruit, you can certainly add more than the recipe calls for.

Combine the butter and the grated lemon in the large bowl of your mixer. Beat until light and fluffy. Add 1/4 cup (50 ml) of the sugar gradually, beating after each addition until the mixture is smooth. Add 1 egg, 1 tablespoon (15 ml) of the flour, and the salt. Beat until smooth.

Add the remaining eggs alternately with the flour, beating thoroughly after each addition. Spoon into a well-greased 9-inch pan, and spread evenly.

Combine the almonds and the fruit, and sprinkle the mixture entirely over the cake mixture. Now sprinkle on the remaining white sugar.

Bake in a preheated 350°F oven for 30 to 35 minutes, or until golden. Do not overcook, but do check to make sure it isn't runny in the centre.

I find that this cake makes at least 8 good servings, and it can be served warm or cold. I sometimes I add a scoop of ice cream to each serving. If frozen, allow the cake to thaw overnight in the fridge before serving.

October

1 _____

_____

2 _____

_____

3 _____

_____

4 _____

_____

5 _____

_____

6 _____

_____

7 _____

_____

8 _____

_____

9 _____

_____

10 _____

_____

OCTOBER

11 _____

_____

12 _____

_____

13 _____

_____

14 _____

_____

15 _____

_____

16 _____

_____

17 _____

_____

18 _____

_____

19 _____

_____

20 _____

_____

OCTOBER

21 _____

_____

22 _____

_____

23 _____

_____

24 _____

_____

25 _____

_____

26 _____

_____

27 _____

_____

28 _____

_____

29 _____

_____

30 _____

_____

31 _____

_____

A Step Up in the World

It seemed like a great deal to us five children when Father traded enough gravel from the pit on our property to fill a neighbour's culvert in exchage for a dilapidated model T Ford. We had never had a car, but instead had to rely on our horse King to pull the cutter in the winter and the buggy in the summer to go into Renfrew, twelve and a half miles away. Before we had the car a week, we went into town at least three times, always in the daylight hours, because the small lights attached to the radiator would have done little to provide light on the dark road home.

Getting the thing started was a chore in itself. It had to be cranked, while my oldest brother Everett sat behind the wheel and fiddled with the gas lever and the choke. Often it backfired, sending Father's arm skyward, causing him to emit a slew of oaths in German under his breath and complain that the car wasn't worth the powder to blow it to hell. More than a few times, he threatened to hitch King to the axle and pull the car into the Bonnechere. He even said once that he was heading right over to the next line to dig out the neighbour's culvert and dump the gravel back into our pit. Mother said that was just idle talk, which greatly put my mind at ease.

It was a hot summer day when I wondered, too, if we hadn't gotten the worse end of the deal. It was a Saturday, and all of us were piled into the Model T for the trip to Renfrew. The car was still enough of a novelty that whenever it left the yard, we all begged to go. I was sitting between Mother and Father in the front, and my three brothers and sister were crammed into the back seat, each one demanding to sit on the outside. Audrey and Emerson won the round, with Earl and Everett crouched on the floor whining that all they could see were knees.

We flew past Briscoe's General Store on the Northcote Road, and Father reached out his window and gave the horn a blast, just to let everyone know who happened to be looking that we were now the proud owners of a car.

We were scarcely beyond the final turn off the Northcote Road when one of the back doors left its moorings and flew into the ditch. Audrey started to scream at Father to stop the car, but he was on a roll, and something as insignificant as a back door rolling down the embankment wasn't going to stop him. "We'll pick it up on our way back," he yelled over the din.

And we continued on toward Renfrew with the car going flat out, probably reaching a speed of 25 or 30 miles an hour! My brothers and sister in the back seat were hanging on for dear life, but neither Mother nor Father were the least bit worried that in addition to a car door, they might lose a child into the bargain.

Audrey asked if she could be let out at the outskirts of Renfrew to be picked up on the way back to Northcote. She certainly didn't want anyone from town recognizing her. Mother told her not to be silly. Audrey finally talked Earl into changing places with her so she could hide on the floor, but it cost her a nickel.

The supplies were bought, put into two cardboard boxes and strapped to the running boards of the Model T, and we headed for home. Father knew exactly where the door flew off, and when we came to the spot, he ground to a halt. Everett was ordered out of the car, and with all our purchases, five children and Mother and Father, and now the wayward door, the old car was taxed to the limit.

Father could have taken the car into Thacker's Garage in Renfrew to have the door attached properly, and perhaps it was embarrassment or just plain stubbornness, but he tied it on with binder twine, put new screws in the hinges, and declared it ready for the road again.

Over the years, other parts left the car never to be seen again. But the Model T opened up a whole new world for us, and Father eventually agreed that it wasn't such a bad deal after all...a few loads of gravel for our first car.

Sweet Preparations

Preparations for Christmas Day were almost as exciting as the actual day. Perhaps that was because it was a lot easier to come up with Christmas goodies than it was to find money to buy presents to put under the tree. Although certainly Mother had to dip into her "egg money" in the blue sugar bowl to buy such things as raisins and bottled cherries and nuts, I don't ever remember a Christmas without tins of cookies, puddings and special pies made long in advance, and then kept frozen in the summer kitchen. After all, this was a time for neighbours to drop in for a visit, or relatives to come for the day itself, and it would never do to not have a special treat ready for the unexpected company.

This rich and, at the time I thought, very costly cake was made in November, and I have made some small changes to the recipe to bring it up-to-date.

Christmas Pudding

1 1/3 cup	light raisins	325 ml
2 2/3 cups	dark raisins	650 ml
1 1/3 cup	currants	325 ml
1/4 cup	chopped candied peel	50 ml
1/2 cup	chopped red cherries	125 ml
1/2 cup	chopped green cherries	125 ml
2/3 cup	chopped blanched almonds	150 ml
1 cup	ground almonds	250 ml
4 cups	fresh bread crumbs	1 litre
2	carrots, grated fine	2
1	medium apple, peeled and grated	1
8 oz	shredded suet	250 gm
1/2 tsp	pumpkin pie spice	2 ml
	Pinch of nutmeg	
1/2 tsp	cinnamon	2 ml
1–1/4 cup	white sugar	300 ml
	Grated peel and juice of a large lemon	
	Grated peel and juice of a large orange	
2/3 cup	corn syrup	150 ml
4	large eggs, beaten	4
1/4 cup	brandy*	50 ml
	or	
1/2 cup	ale	125 ml
	This can be omitted, if flaming pudding isn't your style!	

In a very large bowl, mix all the ingredients with a wooden spoon until combined thoroughly.

Recipe continued, next page

Grease three 4-cup (1 litre) pudding moulds, or six 2-cup (500 ml) moulds. Fill each mould about three-quarters full. Cut foil large enough to cover the moulds. Grease the foil well. Cover the moulds and tie string around each mould tightly.

Place the puddings in large pots, and add enough boiling water to come halfway up the sides of the moulds. Steam large puddings for 8 hours (small puddings for 6 hours), over medium-low heat. Add more boiling water as necessary.

Remove puddings from the pots and cool completely on wire racks. Remove the foil, and turn out the puddings from the moulds. Wrap tightly in plastic wrap, then wrap airtight in foil. Store in a cool, dry place, and they will "ripen" for up to three months, or they can be frozen at this point.

To serve the puddings: Return the puddings to their original moulds, cover again with greased foil, and tie with string. Steam, as instructed above, for 3 to 4 hours until heated through. Remove the foil and string and invert onto a serving plate, taking off the moulds. Serve with your favourite brandy or custard sauce.

If you wish to flame the puddings, pour warmed brandy or ale over the puddings and light with a match. Serve while flaming.

While writing up this recipe, I recalled the year that Mother tried flaming our puddings, and nearly burned the house down! Father started to beat the puddings with his old felt hat, nearly ruining them. The fire was extinguished before the pudding was flattened, but we never tried this again.

November

1 _____
_____
2 _____
_____
3 _____
_____
4 _____
_____
5 _____
_____
6 _____
_____
7 _____
_____
8 _____
_____
9 _____
_____
10 _____
_____

November

11 _____

_____

12 _____

_____

13 _____

_____

14 _____

_____

15 _____

_____

16 _____

_____

17 _____

_____

18 _____

_____

19 _____

_____

20 _____

_____

November

21 _____

_____

22 _____

_____

23 _____

_____

24 _____

_____

25 _____

_____

26 _____

_____

27 _____

_____

28 _____

_____

29 _____

_____

30 _____

_____

Lighting the Way

$\mathcal{M}$other said she had never seen a coal-oil lamp before in her life until she moved to the farm in Renfrew County. "In New York, you just flicked a switch, and the room lit up," she'd say wistfully, looking at the old coal-oil lamps that stood like soldiers on top of the sideboard.

Audrey, my older and much wiser sister, said that just about everyone had electricity in Renfrew, twelve and a half miles away, but few of us were so lucky out in Northcote. How she knew this fact escaped me.

I asked Audrey if she thought we would ever have electric lights. She replied, "Only if some fairy godmother comes along and drops a bucket of money in our laps." Even though I sincerely believed in fairy godmothers, I knew there wasn't a hope of any coming with a bucket of money to our house.

And so coal-oil lamps and one Coleman lamp that hung on a chain from the ceiling over the kitchen table, were the only sources of light when the sun went down and our log house was wrapped in darkness.

We bought our coal oil from Briscoe's General Store for twenty-five cents a gallon. We took our own old rusty can to the store and got it filled from a big barrel in the back corner of the store that sat right beside the keg of molasses.

It was Audrey's job to keep the assorted lamps filled with coal oil, and to snip off the charred end of the wicks. But it was my job to keep the shades clean, which I thought was greatly unfair, since it was the dirtiest of the two jobs. First I had to scrunch up a piece of newspaper and wad it into the soot-covered lampshade, blackening my hand and arm right to my elbow. Once I got as much soot out as I could, I would take the shade to the table and wash it in hot soapy water, and then dry it with a tea towel kept especially for that purpose.

When it was as shiny as a new penny, I would move on to the next lamp, lining them all back up on the sideboard ready for use—and for what in a matter of a few nights would be ready for another cleaning. I wasn't allowed to clean the Coleman lamp, though, because the little sack that provided the light was very fragile, and if damaged, would cost twenty-five cents to replace—a princely sum in those lean years.

One of the lamps was a favourite of mine. It didn't stand tall like the others, but was squat and fat and had a little handle of the same glass, much like a teacup. This was the lamp that was carried upstairs every night when we went to bed. At the top of the stairs, where the banister ended, was a bowl-like wood container that held this lamp.

It was Audrey's responsibility to take this favourite lamp upstairs every night and set it into the holder where it stayed while we said our prayers around Mother's knee. And when it was time to go to sleep, it was Audrey's job to turn down the wick and blow out this special lamp, sending the upstairs into total darkness.

On a shelf at Briscoe's General Store was also a long row of glass lamp-shades. They were all exactly the same, plain glass, and all the same size, so that they would fit any lamp. And then one day, Mother came home with a lampshade that Father thought was a complete waste of hard-earned money.

This one had been etched and frosted in a flower design, and I thought it was lovely. Father's comment was, "Come easy, go easy," which meant he felt the dime extra it cost could have been spent more wisely else-where.

Mother had a healthy respect for the coal-oil lamps when they were lit. Only Mother, Father and Audrey were allowed to touch them then. And she insisted they be kept as far away from the Findlay Oval as pos-sible. "If that coal oil ever came in contact with the stove, this whole place would go up like a tinderbox," she'd caution.

Coal-oil lamps were very much a symbol of the time. Their glow would warm a room on a cold night, and a lamp in a window welcomed you when darkness fell, reaching out like a familiar hand to guide you home.

A Christmas Tradition

It just wasn't Christmas for Father if we didn't have a farm-raised goose on the table. Often Mother would have to do both goose and turkey, because the truth of the matter was that we children much preferred turkey. So on Christmas Eve the turkey would go in the oven, and just before we left for church on Christmas morning, while the cooked turkey "rested" on the back of the Findlay Oval in the large navy blue roasting pan, the goose would be put into the oven to be ready for our Christmas dinner.

With the table laden with both birds, and accompanied by mounds of creamy mashed potatoes, two or three different vegetables, jellied salads, homemade buns, and Christmas pudding and mince meat pies on the sideboard, I would look the rich spread of food and wonder what all that talk of the Depression was about. Surely, it was happening in some other part of the world!

Recipe, next page

Our Special Christmas Roast Goose Stuffing

(enough for a 10-pound farm-raised goose)

7 cups	soft white bread crumbs	1.75 litres
2/3 cup	soft butter	150 ml
I	large cooking apple	I
	(or several soaked and stoned prunes)	
1/2 cup	finely chopped sweet onion	125 ml
1/2 cup	chopped celery (optional)	125 ml
I tsp	salt	5 ml
1/2 tsp	sage	2 ml
1/4 tsp	basil	I ml
1/4 tsp	marjoram	I ml
1/4 tsp	rosemary	I ml
1/4 tsp	pepper	I ml

The stuffing can be made ahead and stored in the refrigerator. In a large frying pan, melt the butter and then slowly sauté the onion and celery until limp. Stir in the apple (or prunes), and then add all the seasonings and the bread crumbs. Stir gently and thoroughly on low heat, until the crumbs crisp. (If making ahead, cool and then store in a sealed container in the fridge.)

Stuff the well-washed goose loosely with the dressing. Skewer the opening to close. Place the goose, breast side up, in a roast pan on top of several thick slices of bread. Prick the goose all over to allow the fat to release. Cook at 250°F for seven hours. When it is done, lift out the goose, and discard the bread slices which will have absorbed the fat.

Note: If you don't use the bread, you will have to remove the fat from the roaster every hour or so and discard.

DECEMBER

1 _____

_____

2 _____

_____

3 _____

_____

4 _____

_____

5 _____

_____

6 _____

_____

7 _____

_____

8 _____

_____

9 _____

_____

10 _____

_____

December

11 _____

_____

12 _____

_____

13 _____

_____

14 _____

_____

15 _____

_____

16 _____

_____

17 _____

_____

18 _____

_____

19 _____

_____

20 _____

_____

December

21 _____

_____

22 _____

_____

23 _____

_____

24 _____

_____

25 _____

_____

26 _____

_____

27 _____

_____

28 _____

_____

29 _____

_____

30 _____

_____

31 _____

_____

Musings

MUSINGS

MUSINGS

MUSINGS

Musings

Would you like more than "just a taste" of Mary's stories?

Here are other books by Mary Cook

In her ever-popular "Thirties" stories, initially broadcast by the CBC and then released in print in leading newspapers and best-selling books, Mary Cook transports her audience to a time when families and communities were bound together by the need to survive. These were tough times for the Haneman family, but Mary Cook's remembrances of growing up on the family farm in the Depression years include even larger servings of joy and laughter.

**Liar, Liar,
Pants on Fire!**
ISBN: 0-921165-40-4
160 pages, trade paper
$18.95

**Another Place
at the Table**
ISBN: 0-921165-57-9
152 pages, trade paper
$19.95
This is Mary
(Haneman) Cook's
tribute to the remark-
able woman who was
her mother.

**A Bubble off Plumb
and other audience
favourites**
ISBN: 0-921165-86-2
176 pages, trade paper
$20.95